Our Young Lady of Paris

Notre Jeune Dame de Paris

Coco Mary

Released by Flower Child Books
www.flowerchildbooks.world

$23.00
ISBN 978-1-7361674-4-1

Printed in the United States of America.

Dedicated
to
Seraph

and

the mysteries
of
the teenage mind

Note from the author:

This book is a dreamscape of the inner world of Agnes.
Her clothing changes constantly, and Paris is seen
through her subjective eyes.

6 Janvier 1990

Pop Swatch

" Shake dreams from your hair, my pretty child, my sweet one. Choose the day and choose the sign of your day, the day's divinity, first thing you see. "

It is the 6th of January. Cold as ice.
She opens her eyes, fresh from a really cool dream,
a Jim Morrison song spinning in her head:

natal chart

thème astral

The first thing she sees, the date.
This is her day.

The old church bell rings. Nine deep chimes.
She closes her eyes, and feels them resonate inside her.
For so many years they have been her lullaby and her wake-up call.

She has two safe places in the world: her attic bedroom where she dreams, and the bathroom - marble-cool and scented. It was designed by the one and only Monsieur Christian Lacroix, a dear friend of her maman, whose Chanel No. 5 perfume still lingers in the air.

la chemise blanche rétro de sa maman
her mom's vintage white shirt

Bonjour Saint Michel.
What will this day bring?

le bain parfumé
the scented bathtub

Le nombril d'un ange
the navel of an angel

Be inspired

This day calls for her special Bruce Lee t-shirt;
throw over an olivaceous peacoat against the frost,
and slip icy-cold fingers into hobo gloves.
Some cheeky boots, or her vintage old-lady shoes?

33 rpm

$$rpm = \frac{r}{min}$$

rpm = revolutions
per minute
r = revolutions
min = minutes

Don't think, feel... it is like a finger
pointing to the moon.
Don't concentrate on the finger,
or you will miss all that heavenly
glory!

Bruce Lee

UNVEILED MYSTERIES

Meet Agnes Fleury. Our Young Lady of Paris.

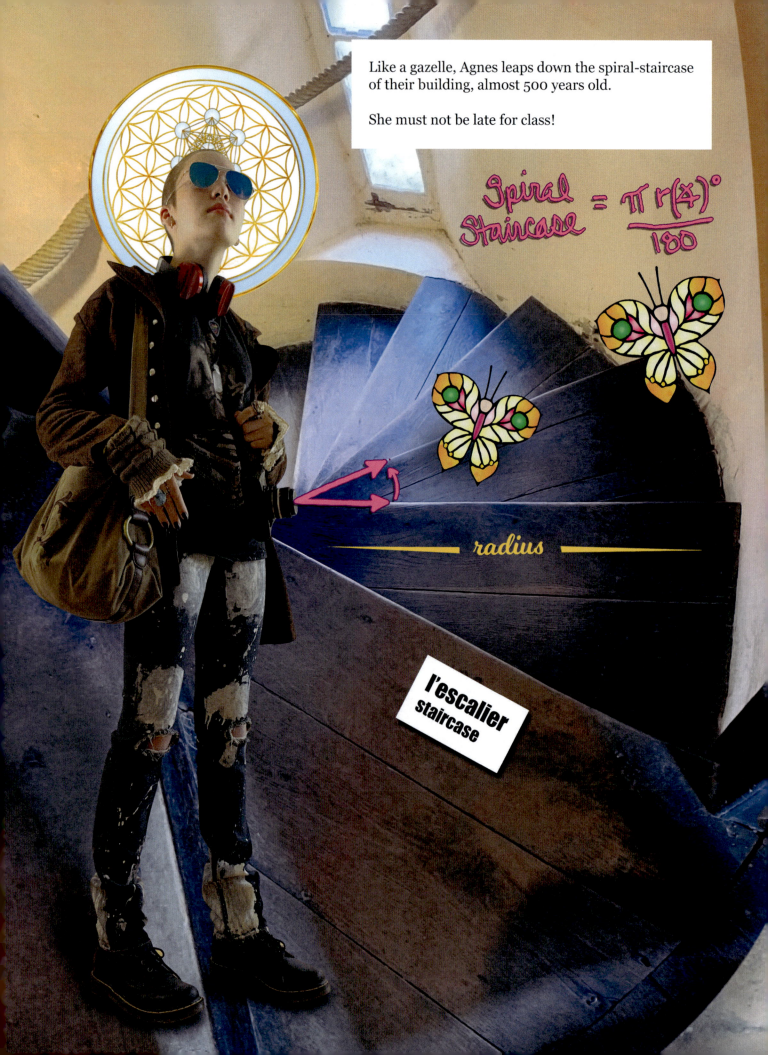

Like a gazelle, Agnes leaps down the spiral-staircase of their building, almost 500 years old.

She must not be late for class!

$$r = e^{\sin\theta} - 2\cos 4\theta + \sin^5\left(\frac{2\theta - \pi}{24}\right)$$

$$C_6H_{12}O_6 + 6\,O_2 \rightarrow 6\,CO_2 + 6\,H_2O$$

papillon
butterfly

At the bottom, she whispers into Saint Joan's ear: "It is our birthday today. I am sixteen, and you, 578!"

This day, this day, is full of butterflies!

Joan of Arc

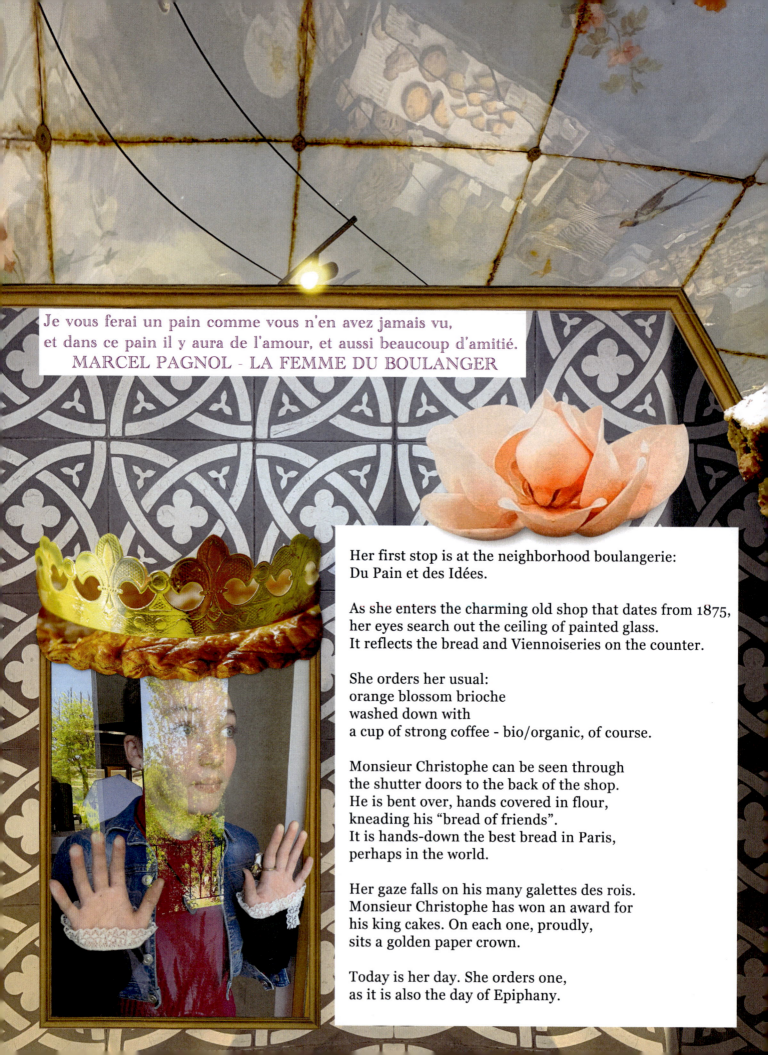

Je vous ferai un pain comme vous n'en avez jamais vu,
et dans ce pain il y aura de l'amour, et aussi beaucoup d'amitié.
MARCEL PAGNOL - LA FEMME DU BOULANGER

Her first stop is at the neighborhood boulangerie:
Du Pain et des Idées.

As she enters the charming old shop that dates from 1875,
her eyes search out the ceiling of painted glass.
It reflects the bread and Viennoiseries on the counter.

She orders her usual:
orange blossom brioche
washed down with
a cup of strong coffee - bio/organic, of course.

Monsieur Christophe can be seen through
the shutter doors to the back of the shop.
He is bent over, hands covered in flour,
kneading his "bread of friends".
It is hands-down the best bread in Paris,
perhaps in the world.

Her gaze falls on his many galettes des rois.
Monsieur Christophe has won an award for
his king cakes. On each one, proudly,
sits a golden paper crown.

Today is her day. She orders one,
as it is also the day of Epiphany.

$$\theta_i = \theta_r$$

TENDRESSE
Pudding aux pommes
raisins et rhum
3,4€

la brioche à la fleur d'oranger
orange blossom cake-bread

Pain des Amis
Bread of Friends

NIFLETTES
Icsime pâtisserie à la fleur d'oranger sur pâte feuilletée, une spécialité de Provins.
6€ les 10
3€ les 5

CHAUSSON A LA
POMME FRAICHE
(demi pomme fraîche cuite dans un chausson de pâte feuilletée... la recette originale !)

3,6€

bio
organic

After having her petit déjeuner
on her favorite seat
by the statue
of Néréide,
the sea nymph,
she takes in
Pont Alexandre III
with its giant
Beaux-Art style statues.

eau
water

Her thoughts drift to the engineering of this marvelous bridge she is sitting on, and its 20 foot high single span steel arch.

As she gazes at the Seine river gliding below, she ponders the structure of a water molecule and wonders how many water molecules make up this river.

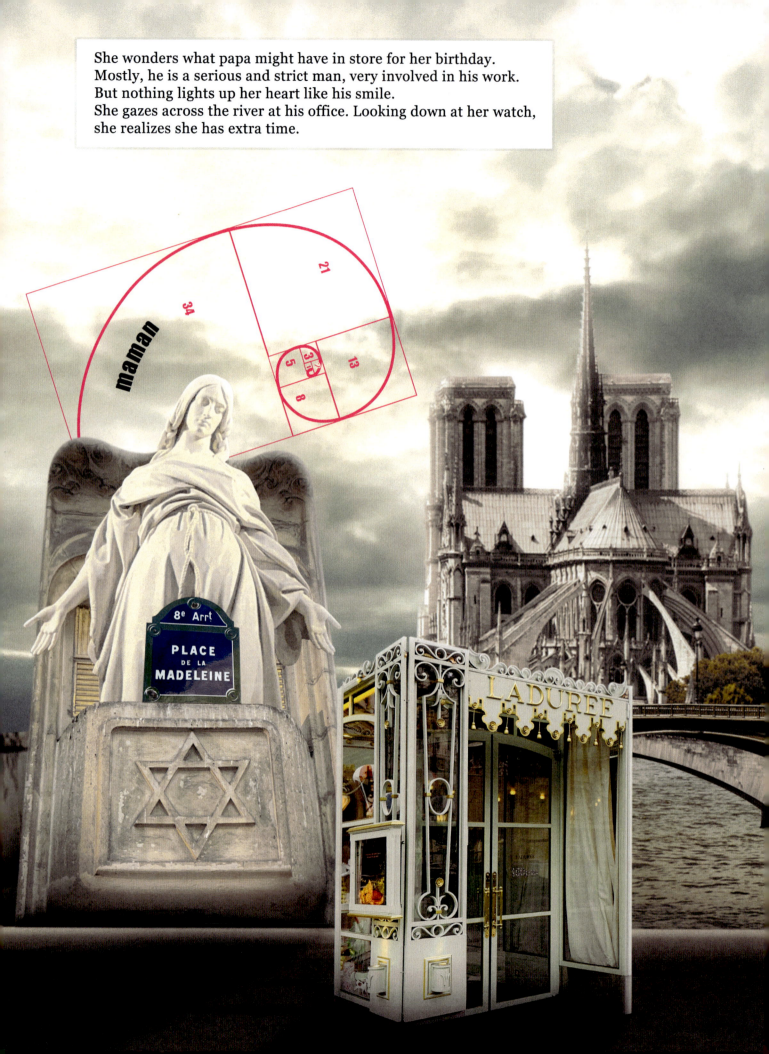

She wonders what papa might have in store for her birthday.
Mostly, he is a serious and strict man, very involved in his work.
But nothing lights up her heart like his smile.
She gazes across the river at his office. Looking down at her watch,
she realizes she has extra time.

Like a child once again, she darts forward and starts to run towards Papa.
The air is brisk and and burns her cheeks. Small wispy clouds rush through her mind.

la pyramide du Louvre
the Louvre pyramid

le laboratoire de Papa
Papa's laboratory

Papa is not at his *laboratoire*. How can that be?
He is always there. Where is he?
And he did not say Happy Birthday this morning.

And her maman is so very far away. The butterflies in her belly are still.

She flees to her close friend.

Saint Michael
mon amour

Trapped in glorious stone - Saint Michael:
always there when she needs him.
An armored archangel, entirely charismatic,
he was sculpted by Francisque Joseph Duret in the 19th century.

As she gazes at the statue, she realizes he looks like a Renaissance
Jim Morrison. A smile comes to her face.

Suddenly, a dark cloud gathers. Agnes can smell rain coming. She digs into her bag and snaps open her umbrella.

$$N_2 + O_2 \xrightarrow{\ \lightning\ } 2NO$$

Lightning

l'éclair
lightning

5.me ARR!

PLACE
DE LA
SORBONNE

As she approaches, La Sorbonne looms. Her 800-year old school gives her a thrill with its egregore of brilliant thoughts, constantly emanating.
As if reading her mind, a lightning bolt strikes right above it. She smells the electricity in the air and it gives her a jolt.

Many extraordinary humans have studied here:

Simone de Beauvoir

LIVRES ANCIENS

Marie Curie

Honoré de Balzac

Jean-Paul Sartre

Victor Hugo

Her *professeur* awaits. As synchronicity will have it, they are studying electricity today. It amazes her that the heart is stimulated by electric impulses, and the brain; like humans are plugged into some vast source of who knows what.

Class is canceled. The professor is ill.

At La Bibliothèque de la Sorbonne she calls her papa.

Come with us. Everything is broken up and dances. Indians scattered on dawn's highway bleeding. Ghosts crowd the young child's fragile eggshell mind. - Jim Morrison

Her heavy heart leads her to Père Lachaise in the north eastern part of Paris:
a romantic old cemetery where the dead sleep, and ghosts roam.
She arrives just as the blessed sun is coming out!
This day, this day.
Give me strength, dearly departed.

She thinks of Père Lachaise - a priest - who founded this cemetery.
She wonders, wryly, why he was called Father Chair.

J'écoute.
I listen.

She always visits the small child,
Adelaide Paillard de Villeneuve.
She was five years old when she was
buried here in 1804; the first one to be buried
in this beautiful and peaceful old place.
And someone always remembers
to bring her fresh flowers.
Agnes digs in her pocket for a treasure.
She pulls out a heart-shaped stone,
a métro ticket and a *bonbon*.
Voila, Mademoiselle Adelaide.
C'est pour toi.

Père Lachaise
Father Chair
se repose ici, en paix.

People remember the dead, but forget the living.

On her footpath she discovers the tomb of Mademoiselle Lenormand:
a famous nun who read tarot cards in the early 1900s. Further along lies Edith Piaf: tragic
French songbird, Colette: who wrote naughty books, Oscar Wilde: flamboyant and even
naughtier, and Chopin, who was a genius composer, but also a wild man.

And of course, Jim Morrison.
Oh, to be so close to him, even if it is just his bones.

It is now late afternoon, and her wanderings lead her to Montmartre, which sits on a hilltop where you can gaze over Paris. Removed from the hustle and bustle, old-fashioned with cobblestone streets and centuries-old cafés and bakeries, Montmartre whispers of cancan girls, delirious painters, and a drink called "the green fairy" that made men go mad in the early 20th century.

Today the magic of Paris feels so meaningless. She feels meaningless. The world is meaningless. She swears under her breath.

mes amis
my friends

Just then the old carousel appears around a corner. With a start she remembers that Papa and Maman used to bring her here on her birthday when she was a little child! She has ridden all the rocking horses throughout the years, seeing herself in each reflecting mirror as she grew older.

Her memories pop up like Polaroids of each child she played with. She tries to remember their names, but it is their faces that fill her heart, and bring a solitary smile to her face.

Chemical Process for Instant Film

(I) $AgBr + C_6H_4(OH)_2$
$\downarrow$
(II) $+ K_2O_3S_2$
$\downarrow$
(III) $+ KOH$

l'enfance
childhood

jouer
to play

Where are those years now?

Bistro

Soupe à l'Oignon:
hot and flavorful beef broth with cooked onions,
infused with white wine, butter, garlic and thyme,
and covered by pieces of thick baguette
over which is poured melted cheese

At a whimsical, but empty, corner bistro, Agnes orders her favorite winter food to warm up her bones. She has a thing for onions, has always had. She remembers how her Maman would wear swimming goggles when she cut onion, so as not to cry. Oh Maman, I miss you *terriblement*. This day, this day.

Tarte à l'Oignon: buttery pastry crust topped with sweet roasted onions and a hit of fresh herbs

Luckily, food is always there when you need her, like a good mother.

After a very long walk, Agnes reaches l'Opéra with its turquoise-colored dome of copper, which, once it oxidized hundreds of years ago, took on its blue-green hue. She stands there and lets her eyes feast. Her mind tries to calculate how heavy this building must be.

Copper Carbonate
$$2\,Cu + H_2O + CO_2 + O_2 \rightarrow Cu(OH)_2 + CuCO_3$$

l'Opéra
The Opera House

The buzz of zooming cars, mopeds, trucks and crazy cyclists swirl around her, and snaps her out of her thoughts. From the cacophony of sounds rises a lone angelic voice through the open windows of l'Opéra. Agnes sits down on mossy-wet steps and listens. It is Mozart's Requiem. She imagines what kind of conversation Mozart and Jim Morrison would have. Perhaps they could write the Requiem of Agnes who lies peacefully in the earth at Père Lachaise, next to Mademoiselle Adelaide.

Her overwhelming sadness alchemizes into a hot fury.

Bitter boots stomp through water puddles as she cuts diagonally to Palais Royal. She marches by the Musée du Louvre and its lit pyramid.

Why do they call it sweet sixteen? When it is more like Fernet.

Crossing the river on Pont Neuf, a sudden powerful wind almost lifts her off her feet. Her butterflies start to quiver and rise.

She hardly noticed how quickly it has become dark. Where were her thoughts?

An old Gothic church rises in the distance. The sky looks unreal. She hears her own breath, cold and hard.

But now ... also another breath. It is behind her. She looks around, no-one there. Adrenaline shoots through her body. Paris is full of dark souls. She pulls her backpack closer.

"Notre Dame is an alchemical book written in stone".
Alchemist, Fulcanelli

La Peur
Fear

Epinephrine
$C_9H_{13}NO_3$

Her shaking steps hasten. She needs to get to the church and its lights. And the people. Marching along the Seine River, the shadows of the trees hang over her. The breath echoes her breath.

She starts to sprint like a gazelle, over the street and onto the illuminated square facing Notre Dame. Not a single soul to be found. How can it be?! She turns around. Her eyes scan the dark trees. No movement.

She hurries into the church to safety. Her eyes adjust to the darkness inside. The air is perfumed with Frankincense. Hundreds of candles create burnt-yellow concentric circles that overlap.

A hush. Notre Dame de Paris has always received her like a mother.

B- Boswellio Acid
$C_{30}H_{48}O_3$
= Frankincense

HAIL MARY

RESIDENCE
MICHEL ANGE

With shaky hands she lights a candle and bows her head. The old prayers she used to pray as a child, and which have long since dried up within her, come alive with urgency. The warmth of the candle light is like a loving hand on her forehead.

When she opens her eyes, her heart skips a beat. Nothing looks like she remembers it. Things feel different. It is like the old church is breathing.

beaucoup de prières
lots of prayers

A gossamer memory from a long time ago, returns. And her world flips.

A soft but sure presence is near her. It casts a warmth on her head, on her neck, on her back, like lulling summer sunlight that dreams.

The air is vibrating. Electrical pulses go though her.
She closes her eyes.

un ange
an angel

She feels her toes lifting off the ground.
Floating upwards, a beatific bliss.
Dreaminess and sleepiness make her eyelids heavy like honey.

Mathematic equations and geometric angles
flow through her thoughts.
She BECOMES an equation.
A small big bang.
Exploding into Notre Dame, she fills the interior with Agnes Fleury.

A thought enters her head from the Presence that is holding her:
You are a localized point in a very large cosmic pattern.
This is what it is to be human.

We are fascinated by your contracted point of view.
Angels are vastly expanded, never able to do what you do, Agnes.

Back in her room, as if still in a dream, Agnes sits down on her bed.
Slowly, she lifts Monsieur Christophe's Galette des Rois out of her backpack.
It is a little damaged, creased and wonky.
She pulls out the golden paper crown that came with it.

natal chart

thème astral

In her drawer, she finds a birthday candle that she has always kept: the one from her first birthday.
She lights it.
Puts on the crown.

"Happy Sweet Sixteen to me".

The galette melts in her mouth. She smiles.
A blush comes to her cheeks as she remembers Saint Michael and her Epiphany.

Her room is a party filled with angel and rockstar vibes.
They move through her body, every cell activated.

Surface Area
of
a
Sphere.
$A = 4\pi r^2$

Agnes's mind is flowering like only a sixteen year old's can.
The world is dangerous to such an ephemeral bud.
That's why she has Saint Michael.

Blood is the rose of mysterious union.

Gently they stir. Gently rise. The dead are new-born awakening. With ravaged limbs and wet souls. Gently they sigh in rapt funeral amazement.

I called you up to anoint the earth. I called you to wish you well to glory in self in self. I called you to announce sadness falling like burned skin. I called you to pray. I called you to be a new monster and now I call on you.

JIM MORRISON

And she will flower with music, Jim's poetry and Math.

THE END
La Fin

Agnes's Playlist:

Jim Morrison	Awake
David Bowie	Starman
The Psychedelic Furs	Heaven
Echo and the Bunnymen	Lips like Sugar
Brian Eno	Baby's On Fire
Serge Gainsbourg	Bonnie and Clyde
Françoise Hardy	Le Temps de l'Amour
King Crimson	The Court of the Crimson King
Peter Gabriel	In Your Eyes
Peter Murphy	Cuts you Up
Jane Birkin	Elisa
Charlotte Gainsbourg	Master's Hands
Vanessa Paradis	Be My Baby
Yaz	Don't Go
Stone Temple Pilots	Wet My Bed
Nancy Sinatra	Some Velvet Morning
Velvet Underground	Sweet Jane, Femme Fatale
Kate Bush	Mother Stands for Comfort
Dead can Dance	Song of the Stars
Edith Piaf	La Vie en Rose
Nina Simone	I Put a Spell on You
Janice Joplin	Summertime
The Cure	The Lovecats

Agnes's Favorite Music Album:

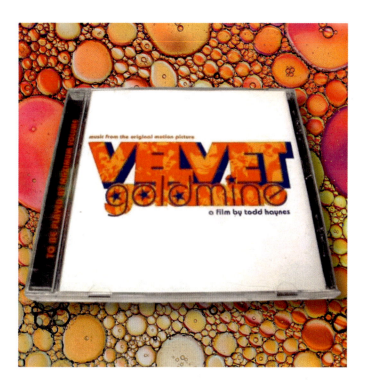

Agnes's Favorite Recipes

French Onion Soup

This is a French recipe. Be generous with measurements. Especially, the butter!
This recipe is for 4 people.

Ingredients:

1/2 cup of French butter
2 tablespoons of olive oil
4 cups of finely sliced red onions
5 cups of Better than Bouillon (best broth ever!)
2 tablespoons of brandy
2 teaspoons of dried thyme
a generous pinch of salt
a pinch of pepper
4 slices of French baguette
a generous portion of Brie cheese
2 slices of Swiss cheese
1/4 cup of grated Parmesan cheese

Directions:

Melt butter with olive oil in an 8-quart stock pot over medium heat. Add onions, stir a lot until tender and translucent. Do not brown the onions.
Add Better than Bouillon broth, brandy, thyme, salt and pepper. Let simmer for half an hour.
Preheat broiler in oven. Pour soup in each bowl. Place sliced baguettes on each soup. Layer each slice with the different cheeses. Brown in oven for 2 to 3 minutes until cheese bubbles and browns. Serve right away.

Bon Appétit!

French Onion Tart

This tart is square, thin and crispy, which makes it a lovely amuse-bouche. Or, if you're a teenager, you could probably eat the whole thing by yourself!

Ingredients:

2 sheets of frozen puff pastry from supermarket
1 cup of Gruyère cheese, shredded
1 1/2 tsp of fresh thyme, minced
2 tsp of fresh chives, minced
3 medium onions
1 tbsp of heavy cream
3 tbsp of unsalted butter, diced
1 tsp of sea salt

Directions:

Thaw the frozen puff pastry in the fridge for a few hours ahead of time. Preheat the oven to 400 degrees Fahrenheit. Place the sheets of thawed puff pastry on a sheet pan lined with parchment. Peel, halve, and very thinly slice the onions into half-moons, keeping the moons intact. Place the onion half-moons on the pastry in diagonal lines, just barely overlapping, and brush lightly with cream. Dot all over with butter. Sprinkle Gruyère cheese, thyme and chives over onions. Sprinkle with sea salt. Bake for 40 mins or until the tart is golden and browned. Cover the edges with foil if the tart is getting too brown during baking. Let cool slightly and cut into squares to serve. Serve warm or at room temperature.

Math, Chemistry and Sacred Geometry on each page, explained:

In our story, Agnes loves to study math, chemistry and sacred geometry. Her mind is full of calculations and geometric angles and formulas. It makes her a loner, and keeps her in awe of the world around her. It also makes her vulnerable, as she does not have many friends to share her interesting mind with. And that's ok. To be popular is less interesting than to have a brilliant one-of-a-kind mind.

Let's see what the formulas and geometries on each page mean:

Page 1:   Natal Chart

The Natal Chart is your birth chart in astrology, meaning the exact points where the celestial bodies were in the sky, at the moment you were born. According to astrology these celestial bodies affect your life and how it unfolds. Because your body is literally composed of the elements of stardust, how can it not resonate with the stars?
For more information and to consult with an astrologer of the highest integrity, you can reach out to: umaruby.com, www.aeolianheart.com and www.ancientastrology.org

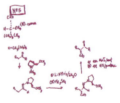

Page 2:   Formula for Chanel No. 5 Perfume

Gabrielle "Coco" Chanel met with a perfumer, Ernest Beaux, in 1920, and challenged him to make a perfume that smelled like a woman. She said that she didn't want to smell like a rose. It was a widely accepted truth that women who were considered to be of good breeding, wore floral perfumes of a singular scent. Racy women wore scents that were supposed to attract men, such as musk. One of the things that set Chanel No. 5 apart from other perfumes of the day, was the use of aldehydes and multifaceted layers of scents. The perfumer took the floral scents of good breeding and mixed them with the sexier scents of musk, and the aldehydes made it last longer, which was good for working women who had long days. All in all, there is no scent that says "Parisian woman" like Chanel No. 5.

Page 3:   33 rpm

RPM stands for revolutions per minute. Vinyl records come in 3 speeds at which they can be played: 33 1/3 aka 33, 45 and 78. The higher the speed, the better the quality of sound.

Page 4:   Spiral Staircase

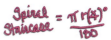

$$\text{Spiral Staircase} = \frac{\pi\, r\left(\frac{x}{2}\right)^{\circ}}{180}$$

A spiral staircase is typically a type of round or curved stair where the steps are connected to and rotating around a center column to form a complete circle. Spiral staircases save space. The reason is, that all the steps are located within a diameter regardless of the staircase's height.

In the Old Testament, there is a reference to spiral staircases being a feature in the Temple of Solomon. This could suggest that they were already in use by around 1,000 years BC. They are very narrow, so that a person could easily ascend into the spires and bell towers of churches and castles. Also, the enemy had a hard time ascending their narrow widths, forced to climb one by one, without being able to wield their weaponry.

What Agnes finds most fascinating, is that one completes full circles by going up and down on staircases, and you spiral like the helix of your DNA.

                    Butterfly formula

$$r = e^{\sin\theta} - 2\cos 4\theta + \sin^5\left(\frac{2\theta - \pi}{24}\right)$$

The Butterfly formula is a very complex mathematical equation using a transcendental plane curve. The first equation of its kind was mapped in 1989 by Temple H Fay. Since then, there have been many variations because of the use of computer programming. The brilliance of the Butterfly formula is in showing that math can be both beautiful and creative.

                    Saint Joan's Halo

$$C_6H_{12}O_6 + 6\,O_2 \xrightarrow{\;\Delta\;} 6\,CO_2 + 6\,H_2O$$

This author feels that instead of being burned at the stake, our beloved Saint Joan would rather have enjoyed a roasted marshmallow, hence her halo with the chemical formula of a marshmallow. When heating a marshmallow, the sugar splits into both carbon molecules and water vapor. The water evaporates and leaves the crunchy carbon outside of the gooey marshmallow.

Page 5:   Reflection in Mirror

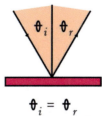

$$\theta_i = \theta_r$$

This is something that we use continuously without ever thinking about it: how we can see ourselves in a mirror, or when driving, use our rearview mirrors. On this page, we see the entirety of the layout of all of the baked goods, not by looking down at them through the window, but by seeing them reflected up. This way, the store owner allows you to see the whole display of baked goods from one position in front of the window. One more reason Monsieur Christophe is a master baker!

Page 6: Water Molecule

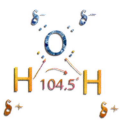

Water is a polar molecule, composed of 2 hydrogen atoms bonded to a single oxygen atom.
An oxygen atom has 6 electrons in its outer shell, but has room for 8. A full shell is a happy, stable shell.
Hydrogen has just 1 electron. 2 hydrogen atoms easily fit into the extra space in an oxygen's shell. Electrons carry a negative charge and by taking on the 2 hydrogen atoms, they make one side of the molecule slightly negatively charged or polarized. Like little magnets, water molecules like to stick to one another. This is called cohesion. It is why water forms droplets and beads on surfaces.

Page 7: Fibonacci's Spiral

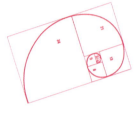

The Fibonacci's Spiral and Golden Rectangles are commonly found in nature and the proportions are seemingly the most pleasing to the eye. The numbers increase at a rate so that the sum of the previous two numbers are one side of the rectangle and the other side is the larger number. The numerical value for this ratio is: 1:1.618, also called phi or Φ.
Examples of this pattern can be seen in the geometry of pinecones, sea shells, sunflowers, tree branches, flower petals, pineapples, cauliflower, etc.

Page 8: Octagram

An octagram is an eight-pointed star polygon. In sacred geometry it is a masculine sign - the sign of the warrior. It calls on the forces of the earth, fire, water and air. The other four points represent the four points on a compass - North, South, East and West. It is an ancient symbol used by many religions, and also by the occult.

Page 9: Lightning

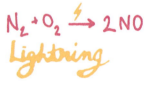

The Chemistry of Lightning: the earth's atmosphere is made up of about 78% nitrogen gas, or N2, and oxygen, O2, makes up about 21%. When we have a storm, there is an updraft of very cold air, ice droplets and small water droplets, and they collide in the cloud with the heavier hail that is falling down. When they hit each other, they release energy, causing the positively charged ions to go up and the negatively charged ions to go down. The power of the newly created ions separating, releases a bolt of energy that is roughly 54,000F degrees. The O2 will split up, some adding to other O2 molecules, forming O3, which we call "ozone". We recognize the pre-rain smell of ozone, but it is also what gives lightning its blue-white color. Lightning ionizes the air in its path. Remembering that the air is mostly N2 and O2, the immense heat of the reaction from the bolt of lightning, causes the nitrogen and the oxygen to form nitrogen oxides, or NO, that dissolve into the rain and give plants necessary nutrients when it falls to earth.

Page 11:   Flower of Life

The Flower Of Life symbol is one of the most fascinating, well known, and recognized geometric symbols in the magical world of Sacred Geometry. Within the Flower of Life motif are found many other symbols, such as the Seed of Life, the Tree of Life and even Metatron's Cube that gave us the 5 platonic solids. These shapes act as the building blocks for all living things. It begins with one circle, but the pattern is completed by the overlapping of nineteen circles. The pattern formed creates an image of perfectly symmetrical flowers representing the cycle of life.

Page 12:   Absinthe

Absinthe is a drink made from wormwood, aniseed and fennel. It becomes green when distilled and has a very high alcoholic content of 45-74%. Also known as "The Green Fairy", it was a drink associated with artists in France in the 19th and early 20th centuries.
Thujone is one of the components of the distilled wormwood; it is the controversial element of absinthe. Chemically speaking, there are 4 variations of thujone. Some are toxic, some are not. In its poisonous state, it causes neurological seizures, hallucinations, psychedelic episodes and a whole host of unsavory side effects.

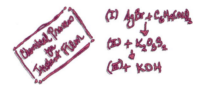

Page 13:   Chemical Process of Instant Film

Instant film! Isn't it fascinating? The concept alone is amazing. The inventor took the chemical reactions that would take place in a dark room and basically recreated it on a mini scale inside the camera, using the box shape of the film tray and contact papers as the dark room. Then, when he wanted color film, he did it again but in multiple layers. Silver bromide (AgBr) is necessary, then each color has a mini layer of reactant for that particular color, like you would see in a color printer, but it is activated by the light of the camera lens. The hydroquinone (C6H4(OH)2) takes the silver bromide and makes it into silver and its colors, or black. Potassium thiosulfate (K2O3S2) is a developing agent that eats up any unused silver bromide and sets the photo. Then, potassium hydroxide (KOH) is added on rollers as the film is ejecting from the camera. This is a compound to speed up the developing process.

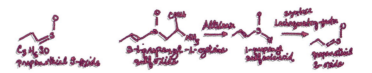

Page 14:   Onions

Why do we cry when we cut onions?
Interestingly enough, the chemical that causes the tears, Propanethial S-oxide, is not actually IN the onion. It is produced when the layers of the onion become damaged. There are a series of chemical reactions that take place when you cut through the layers of an onion. Scientists believe that it is the onion's protection mechanism against herbivores. The offensive chemical is released into the air and causes a teary irritant to the cornea of the eye without causing any serious damage.

Page 15:   Copper Carbonate

Copper Carbonate

$$2\,Cu + H_2O + CO_2 + O_2 \rightarrow Cu(OH)_2 + CuCO_3$$

Why is it that some pennies turn black, but some turn a lovely greenish turquoise color? CuO is copper oxide ... black pennies. The beautiful greenish color that is seen on many old buildings, is copper carbonate. The difference, other than the color, is that the green layer that is formed when the copper is reacting with the elements found during a rain storm - oxygen, carbon dioxide and water - makes a protective coating over the metal. Oxidation is a destructive process and breaks the metal down, whereas the carbonate coat, or patina, acts as a shield, and makes it beautiful to look at, as well as preserving the building.

Page 16:   Adrenaline

Epinephrine

$$C_9H_{13}NO_3$$

The secretion of epinephrine, also known as the hormone - adrenaline (because it comes from the adrenal glands of the body), is part of the human "fight or flight" response to extreme fear or panic. The body's heart rate and the strength of cardio contractions increase, spiking the blood pressure, which opens up the bronchioles in the lungs and increases the levels of blood sugar and other agents that raise the body's metabolic output. It makes you feel "super human" for a short time.

          Star of David

This is a six-pointed geometrical shape consisting of two interlaced equilateral triangles, which was used as an old Hebrew symbol of protection, and still is today. The biblical figure, David, used this symbol as a shield, physically and figuratively.

Page 17:   Frankincense

β-Boswellic Acid
$$C_{30}H_{48}O_3$$
Frankincense

Frankincense is also known as olibanum oil. The main ingredient in Frankincense is 3-acetyl-beta-boswellic acid or β-Boswellic acid. It is created by using steam to distill the sap of the Boswellia carterii tree.
Mediterranean religions in antiquity were rich with olfaction. This held true for Greco-Roman paganism as well as for Judaism. Everybody used incense and unguents in the home and in public buildings; a wide variety of substances were burned in ritual settings – mostly plants, oils and spices, often imported at great cost from Arabia, Africa and India. At a time when 'bad air' was believed to be a cause of disease, perfumes and incense were used to cleanse the air both as prescribed medicine and as a preventative health measure.

Page 18:   Trigonometry Spiral

There are 3 different Trigonometric Identity Properties swirling around our girl, Agnes. Identity properties are things that are equal. Sin Sum to Product identity shows that what she adds can be multiplied to much more. The Difference to Product Identity, is what makes her different and unique, and makes her more. Difference is not always a negative thing. The Double Angle Property is tricky. It is like a roller coaster of higher highs, but also lower lows, very much like Agnes's life at this present time.

Page 19:   LBRP Diagram

The Lesser Banishing Ritual of the Pentagram (or LBRP) is a ceremonial magic ritual that is highly dynamic, using gesture, visualization and the pronunciation of certain words of power, combining prayer and evocation as well as clearing and preparing a space for further magical or meditative work.

The ritual is perceived as banishing any "chaotic" and "impure" forms of the elements from the magician's circle, as she/he traces the Pentagrams in the air and calls out certain Qabalistic Divine names, thus invoking angelic intelligences to fortify and guard the circle.

The principal components of the Qabalistic Cross and the LBRP are drawn from the works of French occultist Eliphas Levi. The text originated as a traditional Jewish prayer said before sleeping, as documented by Rabbi Samson Raphael Hirsch in The Hirsch Siddur [Feldheim Publishing, 1969]. Damien Nichols is your guy to learn this very potent ritual from. Google him!

Page 21:   Disco Ball

The sphere in sacred geometry is the simplest shape. It is also the shape that holds all others. Everything is equidistant from its central point. The unit itself forms in our most basic building blocks, such as atoms, seeds, and our planet.

The disco ball is a sphere covered in mirrored tiles. It reflects the light shone on it, in every direction. It creates a trance-like dreamy ambience in which to lose oneself. So popular with teenagers, and with Coco Mary!

Notre Dame Cathedral

Notre Dame stands on a powerful spot in Paris.

It is said that this majestic cathedral is situated on a ley line intersection. Ley lines are lines that flow around the globe, like latitudinal and longitudinal lines. Interestingly, they are dotted with manmade structures, like churches, temples and sacred buildings, and many sensitive and naturally intuitive people believe they carry along with them rivers of supernatural energy. Along these lines, at the places where they intersect, there are pockets of concentrated energy that can be harnessed by certain individuals to connect with a higher vibrational reality, what some people call God.

Notre Dame stands on such an intersection.

Ancient humans seemed to have had instinctual knowledge of these energy lines, as Notre Dame was built on the ruins of two earlier churches, which were themselves predated by a Gallo-Roman temple dedicated to Jupiter. Isn't that something?

The alchemist - Fulcanelli - wrote an awe-inspiring book called Le Mystère des Cathédrales, in 1929. It was about the mysteries of French cathedrals. He called Notre Dame an alchemical book written in stone. For example, amongst the many biblical sculptures on the central doorway, there are medallions that illustrate each step of transforming metal into gold, which tells us that the architects and masons of Notre Dame were alchemists!

Hundreds of years ago most people were illiterate. In order for them to know their Bible, the Notre Dame doors represented writing. The peasants of France would come and gaze at Notre Dame to "read" her. Tourists have something to learn from them.

And the monstrous gargoyles that jut out from the walls? Symbolically, they were created to chase demons away, and on a practical level, they are gutters to help flow the copious rain that Paris gets, away from the building. "Gargouiller" in French, means to gargle. Cool, hey?

My experience of Notre Dame has been deeply mystical. That is why I have chosen her to be the central point of my story. Our Young Lady of Paris is a word-play on Notre Dame, which means - Our Lady, pertaining to the Virgin Mary.

What strikes me the most about Notre Dame, is the multitude of prayers that hang in the air inside of her. They form an egregore of high holiness that cannot be ignored by any human heart; as if an angel resides there ;)

CREDITS:

Page 1: ——— Pop Swatch ——————— www.swatch.com
Natal Chart ——————— www.costarastrology.com
Page 2: ——— Chanel No. 5 Perfume ——————— www.chanel.com
Page 3: ——— Bruce Lee t-shirt ——————— www.bna78.com
Flower boots ——————— www.drmartens.com
Unveiled Mysteries ——————— by Guy Ballard
Page 5: ——— Du Pain et Des Idées ——————— www.dupainetdesidees.com
bakery
Page 6: ——— Water molecule ——————— Photo 140453719 / Water © Trutta | Dreamstime.com
Page 7: ——— La Durée Tea Salon ——————— www.laduree.fr
Page 9: ——— Sky with lightning ——————— Illustration 124328965 © Ievgenii Tryfonov | Dreamstime.com
Page 10: ——— Albert Einstein ——————— Photo 8641872 / Einstein © Orlando Florin Rosu | Dreamstime.com
E=MC2 ——————— Photo 102589521 / Einstein © Grey82 | Dreamstime.com
Interior Library ——————— Photo 83418789 © Benjo1306 | Dreamstime.com
Thinking cherubs ——————— by Raphael, Italian Renaissance painter
Page 11: ——— Flower of Life ——————— Illustration 91793397 © Sergey Shenderovsky | Dreamstime.com
Page 12: ——— Modigliani ——————— Jeane Hebuterne
Toulouse-Lautrec ——————— Alfred Natanson
Page 13: ——— Carousel ——————— Photo 181422041 © Wirestock | Dreamstime.com

Children:

(from left): Diana Green, Maureen Thompson, Brian Thompson, Marlé Blignaut,
(accordion player: Maureen Blignaut), Chantal Ward, Yvette & Eunice Blignaut,
Edison Park, Vanessa Holyoak (front), Yohan de Silva (back), Claire Murphy (top right)

Page 14: ——— Accordion Player ——————— Maureen Blignaut

Page 16: ——— Cosmic sky ——————— Photo 173842659 / Sky © Frischschoggi | Dreamstime.com

Page 18: ——— Interior Notre Dame ——————— Photo 135170545 © Ninlawan Donlakkham | Dreamstime.com

Page 21: ——— Disco ball ——————— Photo 113577371 © Hannu Viitanen | Dreamstime.com

All photos taken on location by Coco Mary
All images hand-collaged by Coco Mary

GRAPHIC DESIGN BY: K. ERAL YOHAN DE SILVA from Sri Lanka

Biography
of
Claire B. Murphy

who plays Agnes

Claire identifies as they/them.

Claire was born in Santa Monica, CA in 2007 and raised in nearby Topanga Canyon. With its kind people, beautiful hills and endless wildlife, it has become nothing less than one of their favorite places to be. Claire has been playing guitar since they were eight years old, and now also plays the ukulele, bass, piano and has developed a soulful singing voice. Performing music at local events from an early age, Claire has shared their talent with the community.
"Music has always been a staple in my family, with bands like The Beatles, The National, Journey, Florence and the Machine, and Of Monsters and Men, filling our home", says Claire.

Claire has a gift for languages. They have a natural ability to learn and imitate the sound of different dialects. They grew up hearing Spanish, along with English, but it is the romantic language of French that has captured their heart. Claire began to study French with Madame Coco at the age of 9, and progressed quicker than most, taking to it as if they were a native.

It is Claire's dream to live and study in France. Somehow, this author thinks it is destined to happen. Claire has an old French soul.

Biography
of
K. Eral Yohan de Silva

graphic artist of all Coco Mary's books
including this one

Yohan lives in Kandy, Sri Lanka. Kandy is the home of the Temple of the Tooth Relic, where Lord Buddha's tooth is held. The festival, Kandy Esala Perhaera, is one of the oldest and grandest festivals in Sri Lanka during which the Sacred Tooth Relic of the Buddha is celebrated.
How cool is that!

Yohan's favorite sport is cricket and his most enjoyable hobby is planting. He loves spending time with his dog, Lucy, and her daughter, Jessie, but he loves all animals, and likes to feed them.
Yohan likes to travel to some very interesting parts in his country: Sigiriya, which is famous for its palace ruins on top of a massive 656 foot rock surrounded by the remains of an extensive network of gardens, reservoirs and other structures; Yala National Park is a lush forest of greenery and wildlife interspersed with ruins from ancient civilizations; Udawalawe is a sanctuary where elephants roam, and Polonnaruwa, an ancient city that was once the Sinhalese kingdom.

In his down time, when Yohan is not Indiana-Jonesing it, he loves to have a cup of hot coffee with slightly sweet, salty and spicy snacks.

He says he loves his parents the most in the world. What a wonderful man!

Yohan says it is his passion to become a great graphic designer, by trying new things in the field. This author thinks he has already fulfilled that goal. Yohan is a world class graphic designer!

You can reach him at: https://yohandesign.com, and yohan.connect@gmail.com

Coco Mary is an Actress and a Writer for the Theatre, and for Film.
But mostly she loves to create her children's picture books.

She is also a Druid witch.
She likes to talk to trees, listen to tango music, bake cakes and read in French.

Her picture books are for everyone who is still a child.
May that never change for you!

You can reach her at: www.flowerchildbooks.world, or www.rosariumfilms.com

Made in the USA
Las Vegas, NV
10 June 2023